EMMANUEL JOSEPH

Divine Balance, Harmonizing Spirituality, Work, Love, and Ethical Business

Copyright © 2025 by Emmanuel Joseph

All rights reserved. No part of this publication may be reproduced, stored or transmitted in any form or by any means, electronic, mechanical, photocopying, recording, scanning, or otherwise without written permission from the publisher. It is illegal to copy this book, post it to a website, or distribute it by any other means without permission.

First edition

This book was professionally typeset on Reedsy.
Find out more at reedsy.com

Contents

1	Chapter 1	1
2	Chapter 1: The Call to Balance	4
3	Chapter 2: The Spiritual Foundation	6
4	Chapter 3: The Work-Life Paradox	8
5	Chapter 4: The Dance of Love	10
6	Chapter 5: Ethical Business as a Path to Harmony	12
7	Chapter 6: Integrating Spirituality and Work	14
8	Chapter 7: Love as a Guiding Force in Business	16
9	Chapter 8: The Role of Community in Divine Balance	18
10	Chapter 9: The Power of Gratitude	20
11	Chapter 10: Embracing Change and Uncertainty	22
12	Chapter 11: The Art of Letting Go	24
13	Chapter 12: Living in Divine Balance	26

Chapter 1

Introduction: The Quest for Divine Balance

Life is a tapestry woven from countless threads—spirituality, work, love, and ethics—each one vital to the overall design. Yet, in the hustle and bustle of modern existence, it's easy to lose sight of how these threads intertwine. We often find ourselves pulled in different directions, torn between the demands of our careers, the needs of our relationships, and the longing for a deeper connection to something greater than ourselves. This book, *Divine Balance: Harmonizing Spirituality, Work, Love, and Ethical Business*, is an invitation to step back, to examine the patterns of your life, and to weave these threads into a harmonious whole. It is a call to live with intention, to align your actions with your values, and to create a life that is not only successful but also deeply fulfilling.

The concept of divine balance is rooted in the understanding that life is not a series of isolated compartments but a unified whole. Spirituality informs how we approach our work, love enriches our relationships, and ethical principles guide our decisions in business and beyond. When these elements are in harmony, we experience a sense of wholeness and purpose. But when they are out of sync, we feel fragmented, stressed, and unfulfilled. This book explores how to bring these aspects of life into alignment, offering practical tools and spiritual insights to help you navigate the complexities of modern living.

At its core, divine balance is about integration. It's about recognizing that your spiritual beliefs are not separate from your professional ambitions, that your relationships are not disconnected from your ethical choices, and that your work is not isolated from your sense of purpose. This holistic approach challenges the fragmented way many of us live, encouraging us to see our lives as interconnected and interdependent. By embracing this perspective, we can move beyond the superficial and create a life that is rich in meaning and authenticity.

This book is not a prescriptive guide with rigid rules or formulas. Instead, it is a journey—one that invites you to reflect, to question, and to explore. Each chapter delves into a different aspect of life, offering insights and practices to help you cultivate balance. From the spiritual foundation that grounds us to the ethical principles that guide our actions, from the love that connects us to others to the work that gives us purpose, this book provides a roadmap for living a life of harmony and integrity.

One of the key themes of this book is the idea that balance is not a destination but a dynamic process. It is not something we achieve once and for all but something we continually strive for, adjusting and adapting as life unfolds. There will be times when we feel in sync and times when we feel out of alignment. The goal is not perfection but progress—a willingness to learn, grow, and evolve. By embracing this mindset, we can approach life with greater resilience and grace.

Another important theme is the role of self-awareness in achieving balance. Without understanding our own desires, fears, and motivations, it's difficult to create a life that truly reflects who we are. This book encourages you to look inward, to examine your values and priorities, and to make choices that align with your authentic self. It also emphasizes the importance of self-compassion, reminding you that the journey toward balance is not always easy and that it's okay to stumble along the way.

Ultimately, *Divine Balance* is a call to live with intention and integrity. It is an invitation to create a life that honors your spiritual nature, nurtures your relationships, fulfills your professional aspirations, and reflects your ethical values. It is a reminder that you are not alone in this journey—that you are

CHAPTER 1

part of a larger community, a greater whole. By embracing the principles of divine balance, you can create a life that is not only successful but also deeply meaningful and fulfilling. This book is your companion on that journey, offering guidance, inspiration, and support as you navigate the path toward harmony and wholeness.

2

Chapter 1: The Call to Balance

In a world that often feels fragmented, the pursuit of balance becomes a sacred journey. The modern individual is pulled in countless directions—spiritual aspirations, professional ambitions, romantic relationships, and the moral dilemmas of business. Yet, beneath the chaos lies a universal truth: harmony is not only possible but essential for a fulfilling life. This book begins with the recognition that balance is not a static state but a dynamic dance, requiring constant attention and intention. It invites readers to explore the interconnectedness of their inner and outer worlds, urging them to seek alignment between their deepest values and their daily actions.

The first step toward divine balance is self-awareness. Without understanding our own desires, fears, and motivations, we risk living a life of dissonance. This chapter encourages readers to pause and reflect on their current state of being. Are they prioritizing one aspect of life at the expense of others? Are they living in alignment with their spiritual beliefs, or have they compartmentalized their faith? Through introspection, we begin to see where imbalances lie and how they manifest in our relationships, work, and ethical decisions.

The concept of divine balance is rooted in the idea that all aspects of life are interconnected. Spirituality informs our work ethic, love enriches our professional lives, and ethical business practices reflect our inner values. This chapter introduces the idea that true harmony arises when we stop viewing these areas as separate and start seeing them as parts of a greater whole. By embracing this holistic perspective, we can begin to live with greater purpose and integrity.

Finally, this chapter sets the tone for the rest of the book by emphasizing that balance is not a destination but a journey. It requires patience, effort, and a willingness to adapt. The call to balance is a call to live authentically, to honor our spiritual nature while engaging fully with the world around us. It is an invitation to create a life that is not only successful but also deeply meaningful.

3

Chapter 2: The Spiritual Foundation

At the heart of divine balance lies spirituality—a connection to something greater than ourselves. This chapter explores the role of spirituality as the foundation upon which all other aspects of life are built. Whether through prayer, meditation, or acts of service, spirituality provides a sense of purpose and grounding. It reminds us that we are part of a larger tapestry, and our actions have ripple effects that extend far beyond our immediate understanding.

Spirituality is not confined to religious practices; it is a deeply personal experience that can take many forms. For some, it may involve communing with nature, while for others, it might mean engaging in creative expression. This chapter encourages readers to define spirituality on their own terms, free from societal expectations or dogma. By cultivating a spiritual practice that resonates with their unique essence, individuals can tap into a wellspring of inner peace and resilience.

A strong spiritual foundation also serves as a compass, guiding us through life's challenges. When faced with difficult decisions at work or in relationships, spirituality provides clarity and perspective. It helps us discern what truly matters and align our actions with our highest values. This chapter emphasizes the importance of integrating spirituality into everyday life, rather than relegating it to isolated moments of reflection.

Ultimately, spirituality is the thread that weaves together the fabric of

CHAPTER 2: THE SPIRITUAL FOUNDATION

our existence. It connects us to ourselves, to others, and to the divine. By nurturing our spiritual lives, we create a solid foundation that supports us in all areas of life. This chapter concludes with practical suggestions for deepening one's spiritual practice, such as setting aside time for daily reflection, engaging in acts of kindness, and seeking out communities that share similar values.

4

Chapter 3: The Work-Life Paradox

In today's fast-paced world, the line between work and life has become increasingly blurred. Many people struggle to find a healthy balance between their professional ambitions and personal well-being. This chapter delves into the work-life paradox, exploring how we can pursue our career goals without sacrificing our health, relationships, or spiritual growth. It challenges the notion that success requires constant hustle and instead advocates for a more mindful approach to work.

The key to resolving the work-life paradox lies in redefining success. Rather than measuring achievement solely by external metrics—such as job titles or income—this chapter encourages readers to consider what truly brings them fulfillment. Is it the ability to spend quality time with loved ones? The opportunity to contribute meaningfully to society? By aligning our professional pursuits with our core values, we can create a sense of harmony between work and life.

This chapter also addresses the importance of setting boundaries. In a culture that often glorifies overwork, it can be difficult to prioritize self-care and personal time. However, neglecting these areas can lead to burnout and resentment. The chapter offers practical strategies for establishing healthy boundaries, such as scheduling regular breaks, learning to say no, and delegating tasks when necessary. By protecting our time and energy, we can show up more fully in both our professional and personal lives.

CHAPTER 3: THE WORK-LIFE PARADOX

Finally, the chapter explores the role of mindfulness in achieving work-life balance. By staying present in each moment, we can reduce stress and increase our capacity for joy. Whether we are working on a project or spending time with family, mindfulness allows us to fully engage with the task at hand. This chapter concludes with a reminder that work is just one aspect of life, and true fulfillment comes from nurturing all areas of our existence.

5

Chapter 4: The Dance of Love

Love is one of the most powerful forces in the human experience, yet it is often misunderstood or taken for granted. This chapter explores the role of love in achieving divine balance, emphasizing its importance in both romantic relationships and broader connections with others. Love is not merely an emotion; it is a practice that requires intention, effort, and vulnerability. By cultivating love in all its forms, we can create deeper connections and a more harmonious life.

Romantic relationships, in particular, can be a source of both joy and challenge. This chapter examines the dynamics of healthy partnerships, highlighting the importance of communication, trust, and mutual respect. It encourages readers to approach love with an open heart, while also maintaining a sense of self-awareness and independence. True love, it argues, is not about losing oneself in another person but about growing together as individuals.

Beyond romantic love, this chapter also explores the role of love in friendships, family relationships, and community connections. These bonds provide a sense of belonging and support, enriching our lives in profound ways. The chapter emphasizes the importance of nurturing these relationships, even in the midst of busy schedules and competing priorities. By making time for loved ones, we strengthen the fabric of our social connections and create a more balanced life.

CHAPTER 4: THE DANCE OF LOVE

Finally, the chapter discusses the concept of self-love as a cornerstone of divine balance. Without a healthy relationship with ourselves, it is difficult to fully love others or live authentically. This section offers practical suggestions for cultivating self-love, such as practicing self-compassion, setting personal boundaries, and engaging in activities that bring joy. By embracing love in all its forms, we can create a life that is rich in connection and meaning.

6

Chapter 5: Ethical Business as a Path to Harmony

In a world driven by profit and competition, ethical business practices often take a backseat. This chapter challenges this paradigm, arguing that ethical business is not only a moral imperative but also a path to personal and collective harmony. By aligning our professional endeavors with our values, we can create businesses that contribute positively to society while also fostering our own sense of purpose and fulfillment.

The chapter begins by exploring the principles of ethical business, such as transparency, fairness, and social responsibility. It emphasizes the importance of considering the impact of our decisions on all stakeholders—employees, customers, communities, and the environment. By prioritizing these values, we can build businesses that are not only successful but also sustainable and just.

This chapter also addresses the challenges of maintaining ethical standards in a competitive marketplace. It acknowledges that ethical business practices may require sacrifices, such as lower profits or slower growth. However, it argues that these sacrifices are ultimately worthwhile, as they contribute to a more equitable and harmonious world. The chapter offers practical strategies for integrating ethics into business, such as creating a values-based mission statement, fostering a culture of integrity, and seeking out partnerships with

CHAPTER 5: ETHICAL BUSINESS AS A PATH TO HARMONY

like-minded organizations.

Finally, the chapter explores the personal benefits of ethical business. By aligning our work with our values, we can experience a greater sense of meaning and satisfaction. Ethical business practices also foster trust and loyalty, both within the organization and among customers. This chapter concludes with a call to action, urging readers to view their professional endeavors as an opportunity to make a positive impact on the world.

7

Chapter 6: Integrating Spirituality and Work

For many, spirituality and work exist in separate realms, with little overlap between the two. This chapter challenges this dichotomy, arguing that spirituality can and should inform our professional lives. By bringing a sense of purpose and mindfulness to our work, we can transform even the most mundane tasks into acts of devotion. This integration not only enhances our own well-being but also contributes to a more compassionate and ethical workplace.

The chapter begins by exploring the concept of "right livelihood," a principle found in many spiritual traditions. Right livelihood refers to work that is aligned with one's values and contributes positively to society. This section encourages readers to reflect on whether their current work aligns with their spiritual beliefs and, if not, to consider how they might bring greater alignment. It also emphasizes that right livelihood is not limited to specific professions; any job can be a form of spiritual practice when approached with intention and integrity.

This chapter also discusses the role of mindfulness in the workplace. By staying present and fully engaged in our tasks, we can reduce stress and increase our effectiveness. Mindfulness also helps us navigate challenges with greater clarity and compassion, fostering healthier relationships with colleagues and clients. The chapter offers practical tips for incorporating mindfulness into the workday, such as taking regular breaks, practicing gratitude, and setting intentions at the start of each day.

Finally, the chapter explores the idea of work as service. When we view our professional endeavors as an opportunity to contribute to the greater good, we infuse our work with a sense of purpose and meaning. This perspective not only enhances our own satisfaction but also inspires those around us. The chapter concludes with a reminder that spirituality and work are not mutually exclusive; by integrating the two, we can create a more harmonious and fulfilling life.

8

Chapter 7: Love as a Guiding Force in Business

Love is often seen as a personal emotion, unrelated to the world of business. This chapter challenges this notion, arguing that love can and should be a guiding force in our professional lives. By approaching business with love—for ourselves, for others, and for the planet—we can create organizations that are not only successful but also deeply fulfilling and ethical.

The chapter begins by exploring the concept of "love in action," which refers to the practice of embodying love through our decisions and behaviors. In a business context, this might mean treating employees with respect and compassion, prioritizing customer well-being over profits, or making environmentally conscious choices. By infusing our work with love, we can create a positive ripple effect that extends far beyond the bottom line.

This chapter also addresses the challenges of practicing love in a competitive and often cutthroat business environment. It acknowledges that love-based business practices may require courage and resilience, as they often go against the grain of conventional wisdom. However, it argues that the rewards—such as increased trust, loyalty, and satisfaction—far outweigh the risks. The chapter offers practical strategies for incorporating love into business, such as fostering a culture of empathy, prioritizing collaboration over competition,

CHAPTER 7: LOVE AS A GUIDING FORCE IN BUSINESS

and leading by example.

Finally, the chapter explores the personal benefits of love-based business. When we approach our work with love, we experience a greater sense of connection and purpose. We also create a more positive and supportive work environment, which benefits everyone involved. The chapter concludes with a call to action, urging readers to view their professional endeavors as an opportunity to express love and make a meaningful impact on the world.

9

Chapter 8: The Role of Community in Divine Balance

No one achieves balance in isolation; we are all part of a larger community that shapes and supports us. This chapter explores the role of community in achieving divine balance, emphasizing the importance of connection, collaboration, and mutual support. By nurturing our relationships with others, we can create a more harmonious and fulfilling life.

The chapter begins by examining the concept of interdependence, which recognizes that we are all connected and rely on one another for our well-being. This perspective challenges the myth of individualism and encourages us to view our lives as part of a larger whole. By embracing interdependence, we can cultivate a sense of belonging and purpose that enriches all areas of our lives.

This chapter also discusses the importance of giving and receiving support within a community. Whether through formal networks, such as professional organizations, or informal connections, such as friendships and family ties, community provides a safety net that helps us navigate life's challenges. The chapter offers practical suggestions for building and maintaining strong community connections, such as volunteering, participating in group activities, and reaching out to others in times of need.

CHAPTER 8: THE ROLE OF COMMUNITY IN DIVINE BALANCE

Finally, the chapter explores the role of community in ethical business and social change. By working together, we can create businesses and initiatives that reflect our shared values and contribute to the greater good. The chapter concludes with a reminder that community is not just a source of support but also a source of inspiration and growth. By nurturing our connections with others, we can create a more balanced and harmonious world.

10

Chapter 9: The Power of Gratitude

Gratitude is a simple yet profound practice that can transform our lives. This chapter explores the role of gratitude in achieving divine balance, emphasizing its ability to shift our perspective and cultivate a sense of abundance. By focusing on what we have rather than what we lack, we can create a more positive and fulfilling life.

The chapter begins by examining the science of gratitude, which has been shown to improve mental and physical health, strengthen relationships, and increase overall well-being. It encourages readers to incorporate gratitude into their daily lives, whether through journaling, verbal expressions, or silent reflection. By making gratitude a habit, we can rewire our brains to focus on the positive aspects of life.

This chapter also discusses the role of gratitude in relationships, work, and spirituality. In relationships, gratitude fosters deeper connections and reduces conflict. In the workplace, it enhances morale and productivity. In spirituality, it deepens our sense of connection to the divine. The chapter offers practical tips for practicing gratitude in each of these areas, such as expressing appreciation to loved ones, acknowledging colleagues' contributions, and giving thanks during spiritual practices.

Finally, the chapter explores the transformative power of gratitude in challenging times. Even in the midst of difficulty, there is always something to be grateful for. By focusing on these blessings, we can find strength and

CHAPTER 9: THE POWER OF GRATITUDE

resilience. The chapter concludes with a reminder that gratitude is not just a feeling but a practice—one that requires intention and effort. By cultivating gratitude, we can create a more balanced and joyful life.

11

Chapter 10: Embracing Change and Uncertainty

Change is an inevitable part of life, yet many of us resist it, clinging to the familiar out of fear or comfort. This chapter explores the role of change and uncertainty in achieving divine balance, emphasizing the importance of adaptability and resilience. By embracing change, we can navigate life's challenges with greater ease and grace.

The chapter begins by examining the nature of change, which is often unpredictable and beyond our control. It encourages readers to view change not as a threat but as an opportunity for growth and transformation. By adopting a mindset of curiosity and openness, we can approach change with a sense of adventure rather than fear.

This chapter also discusses the role of spirituality in navigating change. Spiritual practices, such as meditation and prayer, can provide a sense of grounding and perspective during times of uncertainty. They remind us that, even in the midst of chaos, there is a deeper order and purpose. The chapter offers practical suggestions for staying centered during change, such as maintaining a daily spiritual practice, seeking support from loved ones, and focusing on what we can control.

Finally, the chapter explores the concept of impermanence, which is a central tenet of many spiritual traditions. By accepting that nothing lasts forever, we can cultivate a sense of detachment and equanimity. This perspective allows us to appreciate the present moment and let go of attachments to outcomes. The chapter concludes with a reminder that change is not something to be feared but embraced as a natural and necessary part of life.

12

Chapter 11: The Art of Letting Go

Letting go is one of the most challenging yet liberating practices we can undertake. This chapter explores the role of letting go in achieving divine balance, emphasizing its importance in releasing attachments, forgiving others, and moving forward with grace. By letting go of what no longer serves us, we create space for new possibilities and growth.

The chapter begins by examining the concept of attachment, which refers to our tendency to cling to people, possessions, and outcomes. While attachments can provide a sense of security, they can also limit our freedom and cause suffering. This section encourages readers to reflect on their own attachments and consider what they might need to release in order to achieve greater balance.

This chapter also discusses the role of forgiveness in letting go. Holding onto grudges and resentments weighs us down and prevents us from moving forward. By practicing forgiveness—both for ourselves and others—we can free ourselves from the past and create a more peaceful present. The chapter offers practical strategies for cultivating forgiveness, such as practicing empathy, focusing on the present moment, and seeking support from loved ones or spiritual guides.

Finally, the chapter explores the concept of surrender, which involves releasing control and trusting in a higher power or the natural flow of life. Surrender is not about giving up but about letting go of the need to control

CHAPTER 11: THE ART OF LETTING GO

every outcome. By surrendering, we can experience a greater sense of peace and alignment with the divine. The chapter concludes with a reminder that letting go is a continuous process, one that requires courage and trust. By embracing this practice, we can create a more balanced and harmonious life.

13

Chapter 12: Living in Divine Balance

The final chapter brings together the themes of the book, offering a vision of what it means to live in divine balance. It emphasizes that balance is not a static state but a dynamic and ongoing process. By integrating spirituality, work, love, and ethical business into our lives, we can create a sense of harmony that enriches every aspect of our existence.

The chapter begins by revisiting the idea that all areas of life are interconnected. True balance arises when we stop viewing these areas as separate and start seeing them as parts of a greater whole. This holistic perspective allows us to live with greater intention and integrity, aligning our actions with our deepest values.

This chapter also discusses the importance of self-compassion in the pursuit of balance. It acknowledges that achieving balance is not always easy and that there will be times when we fall out of alignment. Rather than judging ourselves harshly, we can approach these moments with kindness and curiosity, using them as opportunities for growth and learning.

Finally, the chapter offers practical suggestions for maintaining balance in the long term. These include setting regular intentions, practicing mindfulness, seeking support from loved ones, and staying connected to a spiritual practice. The chapter concludes with a reminder that divine balance is not a destination but a journey—one that requires patience, effort, and a willingness to adapt. By embracing this journey, we can create a life that is

CHAPTER 12: LIVING IN DIVINE BALANCE

not only successful but also deeply meaningful and fulfilling.

Book Description: Divine Balance: Harmonizing Spirituality, Work, Love, and Ethical Business

In a world that often feels fragmented and fast-paced, *Divine Balance* offers a refreshing and deeply human perspective on how to live a life of harmony and purpose. This book is a guide for anyone seeking to align their spiritual beliefs, professional ambitions, personal relationships, and ethical values into a cohesive and meaningful whole. It is not a rigid set of rules but an invitation to explore, reflect, and grow—a journey toward creating a life that is both successful and soulful.

At its heart, *Divine Balance* is about integration. It challenges the notion that spirituality, work, love, and ethics exist in separate silos, showing instead how they are deeply interconnected. When these aspects of life are in harmony, we experience a sense of wholeness and fulfillment. But when they are out of sync, we feel stressed, disconnected, and unfulfilled. This book provides practical tools, spiritual insights, and heartfelt wisdom to help you navigate the complexities of modern life and bring these elements into alignment.

Through twelve thoughtfully crafted chapters, *Divine Balance* explores themes such as the importance of a spiritual foundation, the challenges of work-life balance, the transformative power of love, and the role of ethics in business. Each chapter offers relatable stories, reflective questions, and actionable practices to help you cultivate balance in your own life. Whether you're seeking to deepen your spiritual practice, strengthen your relationships, or build a business that reflects your values, this book provides a roadmap for living with intention and integrity.

What sets *Divine Balance* apart is its emphasis on the dynamic nature of balance. It acknowledges that life is ever-changing and that achieving harmony is not a one-time accomplishment but an ongoing process. There will be moments of alignment and moments of struggle, and this book encourages you to approach both with compassion and curiosity. It reminds you that balance is not about perfection but about progress—a willingness to adapt, learn, and grow.

Written in a warm and accessible tone, *Divine Balance* feels like a conversation with a wise and caring friend. It speaks to the challenges and aspirations we all share, offering guidance without judgment and inspiration without pretense. It is a book for anyone who has ever felt overwhelmed by the demands of modern life, anyone who has questioned whether success and spirituality can coexist, and anyone who longs to live a life that is not only productive but also deeply meaningful.

Ultimately, *Divine Balance* is a call to live authentically—to honor your spiritual nature, nurture your relationships, pursue your professional goals, and make ethical choices that reflect your values. It is a reminder that you are part of a larger whole, connected to others and to the world around you. By embracing the principles of divine balance, you can create a life that is rich in purpose, joy, and connection.

This book is your companion on the journey toward harmony and wholeness. Whether you're just beginning to explore these ideas or have been on this path for years, *Divine Balance* offers fresh insights and practical tools to help you navigate the challenges and celebrate the triumphs of living a balanced life. It is an invitation to step into your fullest potential and create a life that is not only successful but also deeply fulfilling.

www.ingramcontent.com/pod-product-compliance
Lightning Source LLC
LaVergne TN
LVHW020740090526
838202LV00057BA/6142